HISTORY SHOWTIME

ANCIENT GREEKS

Liza Phipps & Avril Thompson

W

FRANKLIN WATTS

About this book

History Showtime takes an interactive approach to learning history. Alongside the key information about an ancient civilisation are songs for children to perform, crafts to make and games to play. These are brought together at the end of the book by a play about a big event or aspect of the history of the civilisation which children can perform themselves, using the crafts they have made over the course of the book as props and including performances of the songs the children have learned.

These icons signpost the different activities:

To enrich the learning experience, music from the book is also available to download online as audio tracks, music scores and lyrics. Visit www.franklinwatts.co.uk/historyshowtime or just scan:

 This logo appears where downloadable material is available.

First published in paperback in Great Britain in 2015 by The Watts Publishing Group

Text, lyrics and music copyright © Liza Phipps and Avril Thompson 2013
Avril Thompson and Liza Phipps have asserted their right to be identified as the Authors of this Work

ISBN: 978 1 4451 1489 7
Library eBook ISBN: 978 1 4451 2533 6
Dewey classification number: 938

A CIP catalogue record for this book is available from the British Library.
All rights reserved.

Editor: Julia Bird
Designer: Rita Storey

With thanks to our model Holly Gascoigne and to the choir of the Jackie Palmer Stage School, High Wycombe.

Photo acknowledgements: Ace Stock Ltd/Alamy: 17t, 17b. M Andrews/Ancient Art & Architecture/Alamy: 6b. Ivan Bastien/Shutterstock: 5t. bkp/Shutterstock: 6t. Dimitrious/Shutterstock: 18b. Faraways/Shutterstock: 11b. FER737NG/Shutterstock: 23b. Vadim Georgiev/Shutterstock: 18cr. Getty Images: 24b. Sergey Goryachev/Shutterstock: 12r. The Granger Collection/Topfoto: 8t.

Cindy Miller Hopkins/Alamy: 23b. Peter Horee/Alamy: 23t. Chris Howes/Wild Places/Alamy: 5b. Constantios Iliopoulos/Shutterstock: 16r. Kamira/Shutterstock: 20t, 21t. Panos Karas/Shutterstock: 14b, 16b, 26c. Georgios Kollidas/Shutterstock: 22t. Patryk Kosmider/Shutterstock: 4t. Perseo Medusa/Shutterstock: 18t. Mophart Creation/Shutterstock: 20b. G Dagli Orti/The Art Archive/Alamy: 11t, 14t. Pollartern/Shutterstock: front cover c. Pryzmat/Shutterstock: 15t. Konstantin Pukhov/Shutterstock: 2l, 4l, 5r, 6l, 8l, 11r, 12l, 13r, 14l, 15r, 16l, 17r, 18l, 20l, 21r, 22l, 23r, 24l, 32l. Bruce Rolff/Shutterstock: front cover t. Kristin Smith/Shutterstock: 18cl. Jenny T/Shutterstock: 24t. Walker Art Library/Alamy: 13b. World History Archive/Alamy: 13t.

Every attempt has been made to clear copyright. Should there be any inadvertent omission, please apply to the publisher for rectification.

Franklin Watts
An imprint of
Hachette Children's Group
Part of The Watts Publishing Group
Carmelite House
50 Victoria Embankment
London EC4Y 0DZ

An Hachette UK Company
www.hachette.co.uk

www.franklinwatts.co.uk

Contents

Words in **bold** can be found in
the glossary on page 31.

Who were the Ancient Greeks?

The Ancient Greeks created a great **civilisation**, which lasted for about 2,000 years. It began around the 8th century BCE.

The Greek landscape is mostly stony and mountainous.

Small states

Greece is a country of rugged mountains, deep valleys and hundreds of islands. This made travelling around difficult and meant that the Ancient Greeks were not ruled from one place, but developed into a number of small separate states based around cities such as Athens, Sparta and Corinth.

The Ancient Greek empire stretched across the mainland and islands of modern Greece and beyond.

Mount Olympus

Aegean Sea

Delphi

Athens

Corinth

Olympia

Sparta

Knossos — Crete

Nation at war

These **city states** were often at war with one another, although they shared a language and **culture**. In around 147–146 BCE Greece was **conquered** by Rome and became part of the Roman **Empire**.

4

Great buildings

The Ancient Greek civilisation stretched across the sea to an area of land which today is part of modern Turkey and the Middle East. Throughout the area, the remains of many magnificent buildings can still be seen, though many more have been destroyed. Some of the greatest buildings, including the Parthenon temple on the Acropolis hill, have survived in the city of Athens, the capital of modern Greece.

The famous Parthenon can still be visited in Athens.

Greek government

The Ancient Greeks in Athens introduced a new form of government called **democracy**, which means 'by the people'. It is still in use today in many countries throughout the world. Democracy then gave all male **citizens** the right to attend public meetings and to vote on decisions about how the state should be run. Women had no say in government, little freedom and few **rights**. **Slaves** and foreigners had no rights at all.

TRUE!

Slaves were not even allowed to have their own name. Instead, they were given a name by the people who owned them.

This **mural**, found on the Greek island of Crete, shows two slaves carrying wine for their owners.

5

Greeks at war

The Greek city states spent so much time fighting each other that it was important that they had armies full of strong, healthy soldiers. All citizens would fight for their country when necessary.

Army life

Greek foot soldiers were called hoplites, from the Greek word 'hoplon', meaning a shield. They packed close together to fight in **formations** called phalanxes. Only wealthy men could be hoplites as they had to buy their own armour, which was expensive. Poorer men served as archers and stone-slingers. Their main job was to protect the hoplites.

Greek battle helmets protected the face, head and neck but made it difficult to see and breathe!

TRUE!

The most famous Ancient Greek warrior is King Alexander the Great (356– 323 BCE). He led his army to victory across the Middle East and into India, until he died at the age of 33.

Sea battles

The Greeks were excellent sailors and boatbuilders and they built fast, wooden warships called triremes. The boats had sharp, pointed **prows** which rammed into enemy ships below the water to sink them.

A **replica** of a Greek trireme takes to the seas.

Ev'rybody Loves a Hero!

The Ancient Greeks admired bravery and loved stories about heroes, monsters and beautiful young women. Sing this song to celebrate one of the greatest Ancient Greek heroes, Theseus (see pages 26–30).

1. Once u-pon a time in An-cient Greece, A land of myths and le-gends,
2. Ev'-ry sev-en years or so the Folk of Ath-ens had no choice, a

Lived a king who had a prob-lem, King Ae-ge-us was his name, he Need-ed help to save his peo-ple,
Group of young-sters must be sent to Go and face the Min-o-taur. Young The-se-us, a like-ly lad, and

Find an ans-wer ve-ry soon, when Sudd-en-ly his long lost son Re-turned to be his he-ro!
Keen to make his rep-u-ta-tion Saw an opp-or-tun-i-ty to Go and be a he-ro!

Ev'-ry-bo-dy loves a he-ro, Health-y bo-dy, fit and cle-ver,

Strong in ba-ttle, ne-ver e-ver Let him-self be bea-ten. Her-a-cles and Per-se-us,

Ja-son and O-dy-sse-us, Now this young man The-se-us Ev'-ry one a he-ro!

Ev'-ry one a he-ro! Her-a-cles and Per-se-us,

Ja-son and O-dy-sse-us, Now this young man The-se-us Ev'-ry one a he-ro!

Family life

The father was head of the Ancient Greek household. All the other members of the family had to obey him.

Women

Ancient Greek women married young, usually at the age of about 13 or 14. Poor women worked alongside their husbands. In wealthy families women spent most of their lives in the home and could only leave it with the permission of their husband. Their days were spent running the household, bringing up children and spinning and weaving wool.

This vase painting shows a wealthy Greek wife spinning thread with a **spindle**.

Childhood

Ancient Greek boys and girls were brought up separately. Most children received no education and were brought up to work with their parents. Wealthy girls were taught by their mothers how to spin, weave and run a household. Wealthy boys went to school from the age of seven to about 15 where they learned reading, writing, arithmetic, music, poetry and sport. Greek children played many of the same games as children do today, such as tag and ball games. Toy clay dolls and animals have also been found.

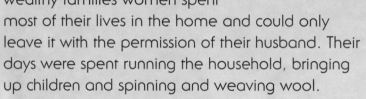

These two young women are playing a game called astragaloi, which was like our game of jacks.

Learn to weave

Greek girls were taught to spin thread and weave cloth to make the family's clothes.

You will need: heavy card or cardboard
- 5 ½ metres of wool in one colour (A)
- 2x3 metre lengths of wool in another colour (B)
- Ruler, pen, scissors, sticky tape

1. Cut a piece of stiff card or cardboard measuring 10 by 15 cm. Mark one side 'Front' and the other 'Back'. Make 16 small cuts about half a centimetre apart along each short side.

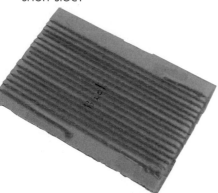

2. Tape one end of a 5.5 metre length of wool (A) to the back of the card at one side. Pull the wool through the first cut on the short side and then wind the wool round the card through each of the cuts to the other side of the card. Cut off any spare wool and tape the other end to the back of the card.

3. Take one length of your colour (B) thread and wrap some sticky tape round one end to make a threader. This is your weaving (weft) thread. With the front side of your card facing you, start weaving 2 cm from one end, leaving a tail of about 10 cm. Weave over the first warp thread and under the next until you reach the end of the row, then weave back the other way, going under the threads you went over in the first row and over the ones you went under.

4. Continue weaving, pushing the row you have just woven close up against the last one. Be careful not to pull your thread too tightly. If you run out of weaving thread, just tie on the second length of colour (B) wool and tape the other end to make a new threader.

5. When you have woven your last row, tie off your weaving thread to the last warp thread you have reached and cut the wool close to the knot. Do the same to the tail you left at the beginning of your weaving.

6. Turn your weaving over and carefully remove the sticky tape holding the ends of your warp threads. Cut through the rest of the warp threads in the middle of the card.

7. Trim all the warp threads to about 4 cms long then knot them together in pairs as close as possible to make a fringe. Your piece of cloth is ready!

Girl Power! (Ariadne's Song)

Ancient Greek girls led very restricted lives. Some, like Ariadne in the **myth** 'Theseus and the Minotaur' (see pages 26–30), may have wished for much more freedom. Sing this song with plenty of attitude!

Everyday life

Although some Greeks were very rich and kept slaves to work for them, most were not and made their living farming and fishing.

Farming

Ancient Greek farms were small. Farmers kept goats and sheep for their wool and skins, which would be used to make clothing. Their milk would be drunk or made into cheese. They kept an ox or donkey to pull carts, some chickens and some bees to make honey. Their main crops were olives, grapes, vegetables and fruit, and wheat and barley to make porridge and bread.

This Greek clay model shows a farmer ploughing his fields. His cart is being pulled by two oxen.

Food and drink

Ancient Greek food was plain and healthy. It was based on what families grew themselves with the addition of fish, seafood and a little meat. Poor people would live mainly on rough bread or porridge. Wealthy families hunted animals such as deer, wild boar, rabbits and hares. Most people drank wine, which they mixed with water.

These wealthy Greeks are being served a meal by a slave.

Homes

Many **public** buildings were built of stone and were grand in design, but most houses were simply built of sun-dried mud bricks with wooden stairs, shutters over the small windows and clay tiles on the roof. Houses were usually built round an open-air courtyard with a small **altar** for family prayers in the middle. In larger homes, men and women had separate living areas.

11

Fashion and grooming

Greek clothes were light, loose and flowing for comfort in the hot weather. They were usually made of wool or **linen**.

Chiton

The basic garment worn by men, women and children was a simple tunic called a chiton (say 'kite-on'). It was made of a length of wool or linen cloth, woven by the women of the household. It was folded and draped around the body, pinned on the shoulders and often gathered at the waist with a soft belt.

Dress sense

Clothes were usually white, though those who could afford it dyed them bright colours. Women wore long skirts and covered their heads in public. Slaves and children wore their clothes short to allow them to work and play. In hot weather, or when taking part in sport, men and boys often wore just a **loincloth** or no clothes at all. Both men and women wore hats with brims to protect them from the Sun. On their feet they would wear simple leather sandals or go barefoot. In winter people would wear a cloak called a himation, which was another length of material wrapped around the body.

Make a chiton

1. You will need: a piece of fabric which measures your height from shoulder to the floor plus 30 cm for a girl, or your height from shoulder to your knees, plus 30 cm for a boy. It should be twice the width measured from wrist to wrist across your outstretched arms.

2. Fold the top of the fabric over by 30 cm. Fold the fabric in half from top to bottom. (See diagram) The chiton is wrapped round the wearer and pinned on the shoulders at points A and B. The open sides are overlapped and can be tied in place with a sash or cord. (See the cover of the book for guidance.)

B

A

Jewellery

The Ancient Greeks loved jewellery and many beautiful items made of gold, silver, **bronze** and ivory have been found. Poorer people would have jewellery made of lead, iron, bone and glass.

TRUE!

Pieces of jewellery have been found in Ancient Greek **tombs**.

This gold and **copper** bracelet, decorated with lion's heads, was found in Cyprus.

Ancient Greek women enjoyed experimenting with different hairstyles, just as many women do today.

Hair and make-up

Women wore their hair long and piled it up on their heads with ribbons or scarves, sometimes leaving long curls trailing over their shoulders. Men wore their hair and beard cut short, or were clean-shaven. Wealthy people, men and women alike, used make-up to lighten their skin as they didn't want to look like sunburned farm workers! Decorated mirrors made of polished metal have been found by **archaeologists**.

Grooming

Keeping clean was important. Greeks washed by bathing in streams or in tubs in their houses. They rubbed olive oil into their skin all over to keep it smooth and soft. After exercising, they would scrape off the sweat and oil with a special curved scraper called a strigil. Both men and women wore perfume to keep themselves smelling sweet.

13

Entertainment

The Ancient Greeks worked hard, but they enjoyed themselves too. They especially loved music and drama.

Making music

Ancient Greek musical instruments included some string instruments that are still in use today, such as the lyre and harp. They also played woodwind instruments such as pan pipes. Favourite percussion instruments included small cymbals and hand-held drums called timpanon.

Apollo, the Greek god of music, is shown here playing a harp.

Drama

The first Ancient Greek dramas were performed at temples to honour the gods, and consisted of poems which were either spoken or sung to music by a group of actors, singers and dancers called a chorus. They told stories of famous heroes and exciting events. Later on as the dramas became proper plays, three main actors played all the parts, with the chorus commenting on the action. All the performers were men. They wore masks to make it clear which **characters** they were and would change their masks as they changed parts.

Greek masks had large mouths to make the actors' voices louder so that they could be heard even in the back row of the theatre.

TRUE!

Actors are also known as 'thespians' after a famous Ancient Greek actor, Thespis of Attica (Athens).

Theatres

Drama became very popular indeed amongst the Ancient Greeks and many huge theatres were built. Going to the theatre was a full day's outing. People took picnics and cushions so they could watch several plays in a row.

Famous plays

Some Ancient Greek plays are still performed today, including comedies by Aristophanes and **tragedies** by Aeschylus, Euripides and Sophocles. Tragedies told stories about events from the past, often where characters had to make difficult decisions. Villains or those who made mistakes were punished by the gods in violent and often gruesome ways. Comedies usually made fun of well-known people and were often very rude!

The huge theatre at Epidaurus was built into the side of a hill. It seated 14,000 people arranged in a semi-circle around the stage.

Make a Greek theatre mask

Ancient Greek actors' masks showed what sort of people they were playing, with smiling mouths for happy or comic characters and droopy mouths for tragic characters. The masks also had hair, sometimes real hair! Wear your mask to play one of the characters in the play on pages 26–30.

1. Draw your mask on a piece of thin card. Make sure it is the right size to cover your face and that it has a large mouth and eyes in the right place for your own mouth and eyes.

2. Paint or colour your mask. Make its features as funny, sad or happy as you can! Then cut it out. Make a small hole on each side of the mask just above where your ears will be when you are wearing it.

3. Tie in some elastic or pieces of tape to hold your mask in place.

The Olympic Games

The Ancient Greeks thought sport was important to keep fit and healthy, to please the gods and to train for war.

Early Olympics

The Greeks held many athletic competitions, but the most important of these were the Olympic Games which were first held in 776 BCE. They took place every four years at Olympia in western Greece. Athletes came from all over the world to take part and because the Greek states were so often at war with one another, a **truce** was declared to allow people to travel safely to the games.

Big events

The most popular Olympic events included running, wrestling, throwing the discus and javelin, long jump, boxing and **chariot**-racing. These were all believed to be good training for being a soldier. There was also a very violent and dangerous event called pankration, which combined elements of boxing and wrestling. There were no rules for this event, except that biting and gouging your opponent's eyes were not allowed!

The ruins of the Palaestra at Olympia. Events such as boxing and wrestling were staged here.

TRUE!

Women were not allowed to attend the Olympic Games, maybe because the athletes competed naked!

An Olympic runner stands poised to start his race.

An Olympic charioteer urges his horse on.

Differences

Some of the sports took place rather differently from how we know them today. Boxers, for example, did not wear gloves but wrapped their hands tightly with strips of leather. Long jumpers held a heavy weight in each hand to help swing themselves forwards and they jumped from a standing start rather than taking a run-up. Relay races were held at night, with the team members passing a flaming torch to each other. The winning team lit a fire on an altar to the gods. The most important race was run by hoplite soldiers wearing full armour and carrying their shields. It must have been very difficult to run fast!

Winning feeling

Winners were given prizes such as a big pot of olive oil or fine clothes. They were crowned with a **wreath** of laurel or olive leaves and became life-long heroes in their local towns when they returned home.

This coin depicts an Olympic winner with his crown made of laurel leaves.

17

Religion and beliefs

The Ancient Greeks believed that all the frightening and mysterious forces in the world were controlled by the gods. They wanted to keep the gods happy so they would be safe.

A Greek temple, dating from the 6th century BCE.

Temples and altars

The Greeks built beautiful temples to honour individual gods or goddesses where they made **sacrifices** and offerings to them. They also had a small altar in their home where family prayers were said to the gods every day.

Zeus

Poseidon

Great gods and goddesses

The most powerful gods and goddesses were thought to live on top of Mount Olympus, the highest mountain in Greece.

Zeus: king of the gods

Hera: wife of Zeus; goddess of marriage

Apollo: god of the Sun, music and medicine

Poseidon: god of the sea and storms

Athena: goddess of wisdom. Athens was named after her

Aphrodite: goddess of love and beauty

Athena

Myths and legends

The Ancient Greeks believed that the gods were people rather like themselves. They often told stories about the gods, their lives and the things they did. These stories were intended to teach important lessons about life and how people should behave. Well known myths and **legends** include the labours of Hercules and the tale of Theseus and the Minotaur (see page 19).

The Minotaur Song

Sing this song as though you are supporting Theseus, your super-hero, as he goes into the **labyrinth**. You could act out the song in mime or make up a rock and roll dance routine to go with it.

Learning and culture

The Ancient Greeks are remembered for their culture. They produced great **philosophers** and scientists. They were also great **craftsmen** and writers.

Philosophy and science

Philosophy means the love of wisdom, and the great Greek philosophers such as Aristotle, Plato and Socrates asked lots of questions about how the world works. Greek scientists made some important discoveries. They were the first to suggest that the Earth is round and travels around the Sun rather than the other way round. Some of the ideas of scientists and philosophers didn't follow people's beliefs in the gods, so they were often very unpopular.

Early medicine

The Greeks knew a lot about keeping healthy and curing illness. A doctor named Hippocrates developed ways of treating patients, based on healthy food, fresh air, exercise and good **hygiene**, which are the basis of modern medicine.

TRUE!

The great philosopher Socrates above (469–399 BCE) made himself so unpopular asking questions that he was condemned to death and made to drink poison!

Archimedes' water pump was worked by turning a screw which pulled water up the pump.

Engineering

There were many great Greek **engineers** and the most famous of these, Archimedes, discovered how objects float and how they balance. He also developed a spiral water pump to make water flow uphill from rivers into fields. Machines based on Archimedes' pump are still used to water and drain fields today.

Arts and crafts

The Ancient Greeks were particularly skilled at making pottery. Their pots were often richly decorated, usually in black on **terracotta** clay, with pictures of daily life or stories about the gods or famous heroes. Greek sculptors made statues and figures carved out of a special smooth white stone called marble. The Greeks loved wearing jewellery and many examples of finely worked necklaces, bracelets, earrings, brooches and headbands made of gold, silver and bronze have been discovered.

This traditional Ancient Greek vase is decorated with fierce lions.

Make a Greek clay cup

1. Use some modelling clay (orange coloured if possible) to make the cup.

2. Roll out some clay and cut out a circular base slightly larger than the bottom of your cup for it to stand on.

3. Roll out two thin sausages the same length and attach them to the sides of the cup to form the handles.

4. Leave your cup to dry and then decorate it with black paint or pen, using the images in this book for ideas. You could use the traditional Greek key pattern used to decorate the edges of the pages in this book, for example.

How do we know?

The Ancient Greeks left behind a great deal of information which tells us about their culture and daily life.

Digging up the past

Many Ancient Greek objects have been dug up. They include pottery, metalwork, such as tools and parts of weapons, and jewellery. These tell us about the skills of their craftsmen, the materials available to them and the tastes of the people who used and wore them. Beautiful pictures painted on Greek pots give us information about how people lived and worked. **Excavations** have also revealed the foundations of many buildings which tell us about how they were planned and built.

This Greek coin is called a diobol and dates from 350 BCE. It shows a soldier wearing a crested helmet.

This archaeologist is very carefully cleaning some Ancient Greek ruins at a site on the island of Delos.

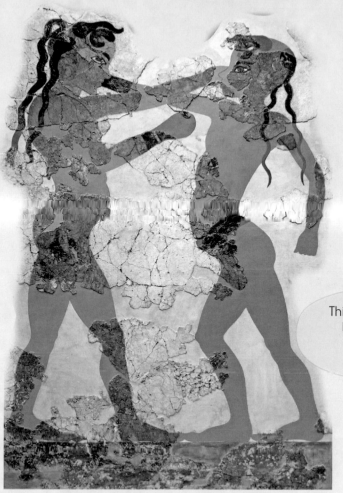

Buildings and statues

From ruins and buildings which have survived, we can find out a lot about what Greek buildings looked like. Many of the public buildings had carvings and statues on or around them and these also tell us a great deal about how people looked, what they wore and what they liked to do.

This **mural** shows two boys boxing. Boxing was a popular pastime in Ancient Greece.

Language and literature

The Ancient Greek language has changed over the years, but can still be read by Greeks today, while the Greek alphabet has remained basically the same. Few original Ancient Greek writings have survived, but the Romans, who eventually conquered Greece, created many copies of Greek books which were then passed on. The Greeks wrote a great deal about their lives, their thinking and ideas and their discoveries, as well as many plays, poems and stories. Many words we use today, such as telephone and television, are based on Ancient Greek words. Some names, such as Helen and Alexander, are also still popular.

This stone carved with Ancient Greek writing was dug up at a site on the island of Crete.

The Greek legacy

The Ancient Greeks lived over 2,000 years ago, but their culture still has a big influence on our lives today.

Art and design

Ancient Greek culture is much admired and has inspired artists, designers and writers. Famous artists such as Leonardo da Vinci (1452–1519) copied the style of the Ancient Greeks in his art and William Shakespeare set his play 'A Midsummer Night's Dream' in Athens even though he had never been there! Grand buildings designed in the Greek style with big pillars and carvings can be seen all around the world, including St Paul's Cathedral and the British Museum in London.

The British Museum includes elements of Ancient Greek design, such as tall columns.

The Olympics

The Olympic Games were revived in 1896 and are still the world's biggest sporting competition. They take place every four years. Many of the events included then are still staged today, such as the marathon and wrestling.

Fairness

Many countries still base their systems of government on the Greek idea of democracy. Our modern law systems are still founded on the Ancient Greek law system, called **trial by jury**, to make sure that people charged with crimes are tried fairly in court.

Many Olympic traditions, such as the lighting of the torch to open the Games, come from Ancient Greece.

A Promise Made

Myths are an important part of the Greek legacy. They were often about what happened when people made mistakes. This song about Theseus and Ariadne reminds us that we should keep our promises.

Theseus and the Minotaur

Greek tragedies told stories about events from the past and about people who had to make difficult decisions. When they made mistakes or did bad things, they were punished by the gods. Deaths were never shown onstage but took place out of sight. The story was told by the chorus, who were a group of actors wearing masks.

Cast

- **Chorus**
- **King Aegeus** *the weak king of Athens*
- **Theseus** *his son, a hero*
- **King Minos** *the evil king of Crete*
- **Ariadne** *his daughter, a princess with attitude!*
- **The Minotaur** *(Say 'Mine-oh-tore') a fearsome monster*
- **The victims** *six boys and seven girls*

Props

You will need the following:
- *Masks for the chorus (see p.14)*
- *A black sail (tie two long sticks into a T shape and attach a black cloth to the horizontal pole)*
- *A dagger*
- *A ball of thread*

Scene 1

Chorus: Good day to you, our audience, and welcome to you all,
We've come to tell the story of a tragic rise and fall.
A hero from the distant past arrives to save the day,
But later makes a bad mistake for which he has to pay.

SONG   ***Everybody Loves a Hero***

(The court of King Aegeus in Athens. Everybody is weeping. Enter Theseus.)

Theseus: What's the matter, Father? Why is everybody crying? What's happened while I've been away?

King Aegeus: It's time to pay the Minotaur.

Theseus: The Minotaur! You mean that dreadful monster in Crete that feeds on human flesh?

King Aegeus: That's right. We've just had word from King Minos that it's time to send him the regular payment of seven boys and seven girls for it to eat.

Theseus: That's horrible! You can't keep doing that.

King Aegeus: Well, if we don't, he'll send his armies back. That was the agreement we made to get him to leave us alone. The group is just about to leave now.

(Theseus thinks for a moment.)

Theseus: I've got an idea. I'll go instead of one of the boys and I'll kill the Minotaur and then we'll all be free.

(The crying stops immediately and everybody looks hopeful except King Aegeus.)

King Aegeus: You can't do that. You'll never manage to kill the Minotaur and anyway you're my son.

Theseus: Of course I can kill it. I can kill anything. That's what I've been doing all these years, training to be a hero!

King Aegeus: But even if you do kill it, you'll still die because it lives in a maze – the dreaded labyrinth. You'll never find your way out.

Theseus: I'll think of something. Right, is everybody ready?

King Aegeus: Well, if you insist. But one more thing. If you succeed you must change the sails on your ship from black to white. I shall look out from the cliffs every day and if the ship returns with black sails I shall know you failed and you're all dead.

Theseus: All right, Father. We'll be fine. Now come on, let's go.

(A black sail is hoisted, a drumbeat sounds the rhythm of the rowers, and the victims sail away.)

Chorus: Across the sea the victims sailed, all feeling sad and scared,
But Theseus was not afraid because of what he dared.
He vowed he'd fight the Minotaur, a hero he would be,
The victims' lives would all be saved and Athens would be free.

But as they reached the shores of Crete all fearing they would die,
They heard the awful howling of the monster's battle cry!
And in the gloom a strange young woman stood upon the quay,
They didn't know she had the power to change their destiny.

Scene 2: *(The court of King Minos in Crete. Enter Ariadne looking out to sea.)*

SONG ***Girl Power (Ariadne's Song)***

(The victims enter all huddled together, except for Theseus who struts in looking confident. Ariadne is visibly impressed.)

Ariadne: Hello! You must be the Minotaur's next meal.

Theseus: Not if I can help it! Who are you?

Ariadne: I am Princess Ariadne. King Minos is my father. And you?

Theseus: King Aegeus's son, Prince Theseus.

Ariadne: (*She shakes his hand, looking at him admiringly.*) Pleased to meet you.

(*Enter King Minos. He is not pleased to see Ariadne.*)

King Minos: Ariadne! What are you doing here?

Ariadne: (*Cheekily*) Just making our visitors welcome, Father.

King Minos: Visitors! These aren't visitors. They're pet food!

Ariadne: But Father this is P......

(*She is about to say 'Prince Theseus' but he shakes his head quickly and puts a finger to his lips to stop her.*)

King Minos: That's enough! Get back to your mother at once.

(*Ariadne starts to go off in a huff, but smiles at Theseus behind the king's back and blows him a kiss as she goes out.*)

Well now, what have we here? A nice little snack for my favourite beastie! He's been craving some juicy human meat. You should do nicely.

(*The victims start to cry again, except for Theseus who is not looking quite so confident.*)

Theseus: Feeding people to a monster? That's wrong!

King Minos: Wrong! Blame your king then for making the bargain in the first place! Or perhaps you'd rather I sent my armies back over to Athens? (*Pause*) I thought not. So you just have a good night's sleep and tomorrow we'll have some fun! Good night.

(*King Minos exits, laughing.*)

Victim: Ok, prince, so what's the plan?

Victim: You're no hero. You haven't even got a sword!

Theseus: Don't worry. I'll think of something.

Victim: Yeah, right! Looks like we're all doomed.

(*Ariadne creeps back in with her head covered by a shawl. She is carrying a ball of weaving thread and a dagger.*)

Ariadne: (*Whispering*) Prince Theseus!

Theseus:	*(Surprised)* Yes?
Ariadne:	I can help you if you'll help me.
Theseus:	Oh yes? How?
Ariadne:	I need to get out of here. You saw what my father's like and he's going to marry me off to some awful old man I've never even met.
Theseus:	But that's normal for girls, isn't it?
Ariadne:	Well I'm not an ordinary girl! I want out of here and you can get me out. And you're a prince. I wouldn't mind marrying you!
Theseus:	So what can you do for us in return?
Ariadne:	See this dagger? It's magic! It'll help you kill the Minotaur. And if you tie the end of this ball of thread to the gate of the labyrinth it'll help you find your way out afterwards.
Theseus:	That's brilliant. Thanks, Ariadne.
Ariadne:	And you'll take me away with you afterwards?
Theseus:	Yeah, yeah, no problem.
Ariadne:	'Cos if you don't, I'll just call the guards and you'll die horribly anyway.
Theseus:	No, that's fine.
Ariadne:	Right, follow me, and don't make a sound.
SONG:	***The Minotaur Song***

(During the song Theseus creeps into the labyrinth, fights the Minotaur and chases it offstage to kill it. At the end the victims punch the air and gather round as Theseus comes out of the labyrinth.)

Theseus:	It's dead! We're safe!
Ariadne:	Ssh, stupid, or the guards will hear us. Come on, we must get back to your ship.

(They exit very quickly and quietly.)

Chorus:	And so they sailed away from Crete, no longer filled with dread, All celebrating now because the Minotaur was dead. But then they stopped to resupply to last till they got back And this is where the story took a very different tack!
Scene 3:	*(The following evening, on board the ship.)*
Victim:	Prince Theseus, may we have a word?

Theseus:	Yes, sure. What's the problem?
Victim:	Well … it's a bit personal but … it's you, sir!
Theseus:	Me?
Victim	Yes. The thing is … are you really going to marry Princess Ariadne?
Theseus:	*(Horrified)* Marry her?
Victim:	Well that's what she thinks. She's going around telling everybody. And the thing is …
Victim:	… she's awful! She's rude and very bossy. It would be a disaster!
Victim:	And when she said that she'd like to marry you, you didn't say no!
Theseus:	I said I'd take her away with us but I wasn't talking about marriage. I don't even know her! I was just trying to get her to help us. What am I going to do?
Victim:	Well, we've been thinking. We just stopped here to pick up water, right? And then we thought we'd stay till tomorrow. So her ladyship's gone ashore and found herself somewhere comfortable to stay the night!
Theseus:	What? Crafty little madam!
Victim:	Quite! So instead of staying, why don't we just head off now while she's sleeping. The tide's right and by the time she wakes up we'll be half way home.
Theseus:	*(Considering)* That's quite a cunning plan!
Victim:	It's brilliant! After all you never promised to marry her, just take her away from Crete. And you've done that. She's a princess, she'll be fine.
Theseus:	Right, let's go.

(The drumbeat begins, the sail is hoisted and the sailors sail away.)

Chorus:	They sailed for home so cheerfully whilst Ariadne slept,
	Forgetting that there still remained a promise to be kept.
	As King Aegeus watched for them, the ship came into sight,
	But then he saw to his dismay the sails were black, not white!
	And so he jumped into the sea and drowned because he thought
	That Theseus had not survived the battle that he fought.
	His death became the punishment that Theseus had to bear
	The tragic ending to our tale of triumph and despair.

Song 4	***A Promise Made***